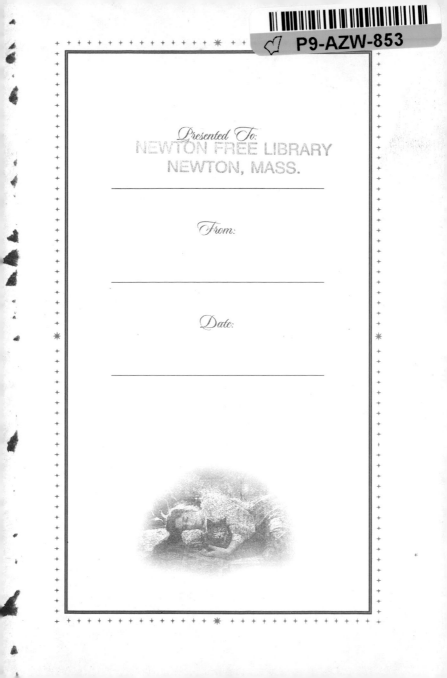

P9-AZW-853

The Quiet Little Woman

Tilly's Christmas

Rosa's Tale

Three Enchanting Christmas Stories

*

by

Louisa May Alcott

Illustrations by C. Michael Dudash

HB HONOR BOOKS

HONOR BOOKS

Tulsa, Oklahoma

The Quiet Little Woman
Tilly's Christmas
Rosa's Tale
Three Enchanting Christmas Stories by Louisa May Alcott

3rd Printing

ISBN 1-56292-616-0

Copyright ©1999 by Stephen W. Hines

Published by Honor Books
P.O. Box 55388
Tulsa, Oklahoma 74155

Book design by Koechel Peterson & Associates
Illustrations by C. Michael Dudash

TABLE OF CONTENTS

✳

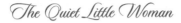

✳

INTRODUCTION

✳

"I LIKE TO HELP WOMEN HELP THEMSELVES, as that is, in my opinion, the best way to settle the 'woman' question. Whatever we can do and do well, we have a right to. I don't think anyone will deny us. So best wishes for the success of *Little Things* and its brave young proprietors."

The words above were written by Louisa May Alcott to Carrie, Maggie, Nellie, Emma, and Helen Lukens on the founding of their home-produced magazine called *Little Things*.

These young girls from an impoverished Massachusetts family were merely imitating the March young women from Miss Alcott's famous work *Little Women*. Those who have read *Little Women* or seen the movie versions of this excellent book may recall that the March girls occupied their imaginations by putting out a family paper of their own called the *Pickwick Portfolio*.

In the *Portfolio*, each daughter—Meg, Jo, Beth, and Amy—was to offer her contributions to this entirely in-house publication. Of course,

✳

we know that the March family could not have sent their paper out to the neighbors, at least not in any quantity, because it was written by hand using goose quill pens.

Miss Alcott, in her letter to the Lukens girls, was congratulating them on something even she and the March family had been unable to accomplish. The Lukens had actually managed to find a printer for their little publication and were building its circulation, first among friends and relatives, and later to such famous people as herself, Senator Charles Sumner, songwriter Julia Ward Howe ("Battle Hymn of the Republic"), abolitionist Wendell Phillips, and poet John Greenleaf Whittier, among others.

All in all, the Lukens girls were so successful with their paper that it became something of a burden, but not before fulfilling its purpose as stated in their poem from the second issue of their publication. Reprinted from a then-contemporary collection called *Melodies for Children*, this poem states in part:

*

A spider is a little thing,
But once a spider saved a king;
The little bees are wiser far
Then buffaloes or lions are . . .
A little pen may write a word
By which a nation shall be stirred.
A little money, wisely spent,
A world of sorrow may prevent;
A little counsel, rightly given,
May lift a sinful soul to Heaven . . .
A little fault, if left to grow,
An emperor may overthrow;
A little word but spoke in jest,
May rob your neighbor of his rest;
A little selfishness and pride
The kindest household may divide.
Little vices many times
Out-Herod felonies and crimes;
And little virtues in the sum
Great excellencies do become.

✳

When circulation reached a thousand sub-
scribers, even five industrious girls couldn't
keep *Little Things* going, and they sold off the
subscription list. Certainly, their efforts had
not been in vain. *Little Things* had given them a
unique platform from which to express their
creativity and moral vision; and they had had
a rare opportunity to live out a dream inspired
by their heroine, Louisa May Alcott.

As for Miss Alcott, she wrote many
encouraging letters to the Lukens girls and
even sent them her picture. She was mildly
amused when the girls reacted to her photograph with surprise that she was not the young
woman they had envisioned. In one of her letters, Louisa Alcott wrote: "I send you the last
photograph I have. Not very good, but you
can't make a Venus out of a tired old lady."

Miss Alcott's attentions to the five girls is
all the more remarkable for the fact that she
was in the midst of a very busy writing career
that sometimes put great stress on her physical

strength. Having suffered mercury poisoning early in the Civil War, Louisa's strength had never been robust since then; but her interest in these young women was so great that, at a time when her stories were commanding prices of several hundred dollars apiece, she wrote several special stories for *Little Things*, "for love—not for money" as she put it.

This then is how the stories we have included came to be. It was, as Miss Alcott said, a gift of love. We hope you will accept this offering from one of the world's great writers with the same thankfulness expressed by the Lukens girls.

Stephen W. Hines

The Quiet Little Woman

The
Orphanage

P atty stood at the window looking thoughtfully down at a group of girls playing in the yard below. All had cropped heads, all wore brown gowns with blue aprons, and all were orphans like herself. Some were pretty and some plain, some rosy and gay, some pale and feeble, but all seemed to be happy and having a good time in spite of many hardships.

More than once, one of the girls nodded and beckoned to Patty, but she shook her head decidedly and continued to stand listlessly watching and thinking to herself with a child's impatient spirit—

Oh, if someone would only come and take me away!

I'm so tired of living here and I don't think I can bear it much longer.

Poor Patty might well wish for a change; she had been in the orphanage ever since she could remember. And though everyone was very kind to her, she was heartily tired of the place and longed to find a home.

Getting Adopted

At the orphanage, the children were taught and cared for until they were old enough to help themselves, then they were adopted or went to work as servants. Now and then, some forlorn child was claimed by family. And once the relatives of a little girl named Katy proved to be rich and generous people who came for her in a fine carriage, treated all the other girls in honor of the happy day, and from time to time, let Katy visit them with arms full of gifts for her former playmates and friends.

Katy's situation made a great stir in the orphanage, and the children never tired of talking about it and telling it to newcomers as a sort of modern-day fairy tale. For a time, each hoped to be claimed in the same way, and listening to stories of what they would do when their turn came was a favorite amusement.

By and by, Katy ceased to come, and gradually new girls took the places of those who had left. Eventually, Katy's good fortune was forgotten by all but Patty. To her, it remained a splendid possibility, and she comforted her loneliness by dreaming of the day her "folks" would come for her and bear her away to a future of luxury and pleasure, rest and love. But year after year, no one came for Patty, who worked and waited as others were chosen and she was left to the many duties and few pleasures of her dull life.

People who came for pets chose the pretty, little ones; and those who wanted servants took the tall, strong, merry-faced girls, who spoke up brightly and promised to learn to do anything required of them. Patty's pale face, short figure with one shoulder higher than the other, and shy ways limited her opportunities. She was not ill now, but looked so, and was a sober, quiet little woman at the age of thirteen.

The good matron often recommended Patty as a neat, capable, and gentle little person, but no one seemed to want her, and after every failure, her heart grew heavier and her face sadder, for the thought of spending the rest of her life there in the orphanage was unbearable.

No one guessed what a world of hopes and thoughts and feelings lay hidden beneath that blue pinafore, what dreams this solitary child enjoyed, or what a hungry, aspiring young soul lived in her crooked little body.

But God knew, and when the time came, He remembered Patty and sent her the help she so desperately needed. Sometimes when we least expect it, a small cross proves a lovely crown, a seemingly unimportant event becomes a lifelong experience, or a stranger becomes a friend.

+ + + + + + + + + + + + + ✳ + + + + + + + + + + + + +

Aunt Jane

It happened so now, for as Patty said aloud with a great sigh, "I don't think I can bear it any longer!" a hand touched her shoulder and a voice said gently—

"Bear what, my child?"

The touch was so light and the voice so kind that Patty answered before she had time to feel shy.

"Living here, ma'am, and never being chosen as the other girls are."

"Tell me all about it, dear. I'm waiting for my sister, and I'd like to hear your troubles," the kindly woman said, sitting down in the window seat and drawing Patty beside her. She was not young, or pretty or finely dressed. She was instead a gray-haired woman dressed in plain black, but her eyes were so cheerful and her voice so soothing that Patty felt at ease in a minute and nestled up to her as she shared her little woes in a few simple words.

"You don't know anything about your parents?" asked the lady.

"No, ma'am. I was left here as a baby without even a name pinned to me, and no one has come to find me. But I shouldn't wonder if they did come even now, so I keep ready all the time and work as hard as I can so they won't be ashamed of me, for I guess my folks is respectable," Patty replied, lifting her head with an air of pride that made the lady ask with a smile:

"What makes you think so?"

"Well, I heard the matron tell the lady who chose Nelly Brian, that she always thought I came of high folks because I was so different from the others, and my ways was nice, and my feet so small—see if they ain't"—and slipping them out of the rough shoes she wore, Patty held up two slender, little feet with the arched insteps that tell of good birth.

Miss Murray—for that was her name—laughed right out loud at the innocent vanity of the poor child, and said heartily, "They are small, and so are your hands in spite of work. Your hair is fine, your eyes are soft and clear, and you are a good child I'm sure, which is best of all."

Pleased and touched by the praise that is so pleasant to us all, yet half ashamed of herself, Patty blushed and smiled, put on her shoes, and said with unusual animation—

"I'm pretty good, I believe, and I know I'd be much better if I could only get out. I do so long to see trees and grass, and sit in the sun, and listen to the birds. I'd work real hard and be happy if I could live in the country."

"What can you do?" asked Miss Murray, stroking Patty's smooth head and looking down into the wistful eyes fixed upon her.

+ + + + + + + + + + + + + ✳ + + + + + + + + + + + + +

Modestly, but with a flutter of hope in her heart, Patty recited her domestic accomplishments. It was a good list for a thirteen-year-old, for Patty had been working hard for so long that she had become unusually clever at all sorts of housework as well as needlework.

As she ended, she asked timidly, "Did you come for a girl, ma'am?"

"My sister-in-law, Mrs. Murray, did, but she found one she likes and is going to take her on trial." Her answer caused the light to fade from Patty's eyes and the hope to die in her heart.

"Who is it, please?" she asked.

"Lizzie Brown, a tall, nice-looking girl of fourteen."

"You won't like her, I know, for Lizzie is a real—" There Patty stopped short, turned red, and looked down as if ashamed to meet the keen, kind eyes fixed on her.

"A real what?"

"Please, ma'am, don't ask. It was mean of me to say that, and I mustn't go on. Lizzie can't help being good with you, and I am glad she has a chance to go away."

Aunt Jane Murray asked no more questions, but she noted the little glimpse of character, and tried to brighten Patty's mood by talking about something of interest to her.

"Suppose your 'folks,' as you say, never come for you, and you never find your fortune as some girls do, can't you make friends and fortune for yourself?"

"How can I?" questioned Patty, wonderingly.

"By cheerfully taking whatever comes, by being helpful and affectionate to all, and by wasting no time dreaming about what may happen, but bravely making each day a comfort and a pleasure to yourself and others. Can you do that?"

"I can try, ma'am," answered Patty, meekly.

"I wish you would, and when I come again, you can tell me how you are doing. I believe you will succeed, and when you do, you will have found for yourself a fine fortune and confident certainty of your friends. Now I must go. Cheer up, deary, your turn will come one day."

With a kiss that won Patty's heart, Miss Murray went away, casting more than one look of pity at the small figure sobbing in the window seat, with a blue pinafore over her face.

This disappointment was doubly hard for Patty because Lizzie was not a good girl and to her mind, did not deserve such good fortune. Besides, Patty had taken a great fancy to the lady who spoke so kindly to her.

For a week after this, she went about her work with a sad face, and all her daydreams were of living with Miss Jane Murray in the country.

A Chance at Last

Monday afternoon, as Patty stood sprinkling clothes for ironing, one of the girls burst in, saying all in a breath—

"Patty! Someone has come for you at last, and you are to go right up to the parlor. It's Mrs. Murray. She brought Liz back 'cause she told fibs and was lazy. Liz is as mad as hops, for it is a real nice place with cows and pigs and chickens and children, and the work ain't hard and she wanted to stay. Do hurry, and don't stand staring at me that way."

"It can't be me—no one ever wants me—it's some mistake—" stammered Patty, who was so startled and excited that she did not know what to say or do.

"It's no mistake," the girl insisted. "Mrs. Murray won't have anyone but you, and the matron says you are to come right up. Go along—I'll finish here. I'm so glad you have your chance at last!" And with a good-natured hug, the girl pushed Patty out of the kitchen.

In a few minutes, Patty came flying back in a twitter of delight to report that she was leaving at once and must say goodbye. Everyone was pleased, and when the flurry was over, the carriage drove away with the happiest little girl you have ever seen riding inside, for at last someone did want her. Patty had found a place.

How Things Went

During the first year Patty lived with the Murrays, they found her to be industrious, docile, and faithful—and yet she was not happy and had not found with them all she expected. They were kind to her, providing plenty of food and not too much work. They clothed her comfortably, let her go to church, and did not scold her very often. But no one showed that they loved her, no one praised her efforts, no one seemed to think that she had any hope or wish beyond her daily work; and no one saw in the shy, quiet little maiden a lonely, tenderhearted girl longing for a crumb of the love so freely given to the children of the home.

The Murrays were busy people with a large farm to care for. The master and his oldest son were hard at it all summer. Mrs. Murray was a brisk, smart housewife who "flew 'round" herself and expected others to do the same. Pretty Ella, the daughter, was about Patty's age and busy with her school, her little pleasures, and all the bright plans young girls love and live for. Two or three small lads rioted about the house making much work and doing very little.

One of these boys was lame, and this fact seemed to establish a sort of friendly understanding between him and Patty. In truth, he was the only one who ever expressed any regard for her. She was very good to him, always ready to help, always patient with his fretfulness, and always quick to understand his sensitive nature.

"She's only a servant, a charity girl who works for her board and wears my old clothes. She's good enough in her place, but of course she can't expect to be like one of us," Ella once said to a young friend—and Patty heard her.

"Only a servant. . . ." That was the hard part, and it never occurred to anyone to make it softer, so Patty plodded on, still hoping and dreaming about friends and fortune.

Had it not been for Aunt Jane, the child might not have gotten on at all. But Miss Murray never forgot her, even though she lived twenty miles away and seldom came to the farm. She wrote once a month and never failed to include a little note to Patty, which she fully expected would be answered.

Patty wrote a neat reply, which was very stiff and short at first. But after a time, she quite poured out her heart to this one friend who sent her encouraging words, cheered her with praise now and then, and made her anxious to be all Miss Jane seemed to expect. No one in the house took much notice of this correspondence, for Aunt Jane was considered "odd," and Patty posted her replies with the stamps her friend provided. This was Patty's anchor in her little sea of troubles, and she

+ + + + + + + + + + + + + ✳ + + + + + + + + + + + + +

clung to it, hoping for the day when she had earned such a beautiful reward that she would be allowed to go and live with Miss Murray.

A Christmas Gathering

C hristmas was coming and the family was filled with great anticipation, for they intended to spend the day at Aunt Jane's and bring her home for dinner and a dance the next day. For a week beforehand, Mrs. Murray flew 'round with more than her accustomed speed, and Patty trotted about from morning till night, lending a hand to all the most disagreeable jobs. Ella did the light, pretty work, and spent much time fussing over her new dress and the gifts she was making for the boys.

When everything was done at last, Mrs. Murray declared that she would drop if she had another thing to do but go to Jane's and rest.

Patty had lived on the hope of going with them, but nothing was said about it. At last, they all trooped gaily away to the station, leaving her to take care of the house and see that the cat did not touch one of the dozen pies carefully stored in the pantry.

Patty kept up bravely until they were gone, then she sat down like Cinderella, and cried and cried until she could cry no more. It certainly did seem as if she were never to have any fun and no fairy godmother came to help her. The shower of tears did her good, and she went about her work with a meek, patient face that would have touched a heart of stone.

All the morning she worked to finish the odd jobs left for her to do, and in the afternoon, as the only approach to the holiday she dared venture, Patty sat at the parlor window and watched other people go to and fro, intent on merry-making in which she had no part.

Her only pleasant little task was that of arranging gifts for the small boys. Miss Jane had given her a bit of money now and then, and out of her meager store, the loving child had made presents for the lads—poor ones certainly, but full of good will and the desire to win some affection in return.

The family did not return as early as she had expected, which made the evening seem very long. Patty got out her treasure box and sitting on the warm kitchen hearth, tried to amuse herself while the wind howled outside and the snow fell fast.

Aunt Jane Takes Action

When Aunt Jane welcomed the family, her first word, as she emerged from a chaos of small boys' arms and legs, was "Why, where is Patty?"

"At home, of course; where else would she be?" answered Mrs. Murray.

"Here with you. I said 'all come' in my letter; didn't you understand it?"

"Goodness, Jane, you didn't mean to bring her, too, I hope."

"Yes, I did, and I'm quite disappointed. I'd go and get her myself if I had the time."

Miss Jane knit her brows and looked vexed, and Ella laughed at the idea of a servant girl going on holiday with the family.

"It can't be helped now, so we'll say no more and make it up to Patty tomorrow if we can." Aunt Jane smiled her own pleasant smile and kissed the little lads all round as if to sweeten her temper as soon as possible.

They had a capital time and no one observed that Aunty, now and then, directed the conversation to Patty by asking a question about her or picking up on every little hint dropped by the boys concerning her patience and kindness.

At last, Mrs. Murray said, as she sat resting with a cushion at her back, a stool at her feet, and a cup of tea steaming deliciously under her nose, "Afraid to leave her there in charge? Oh, dear, no. I've entire confidence in her, and she is equal to taking care of the house for a week if need be. On the whole, Jane, I consider her a pretty promising girl. She isn't very quick, but she is faithful, steady, and honest as daylight."

"High praise from you, Maria; I hope she knows your good opinion of her."

"No, indeed! It wouldn't do to pamper a girl's

pride by praising her. I say, 'Very well, Patty' when I'm satisfied, and that's quite enough."

"Ah, but you wouldn't be satisfied if George only said, 'Very well, Maria' when you had done your very best to please him in some way."

"That's a different thing," began Mrs. Murray, but Miss Jane shook her head and Ella said, laughing—

"It's no use to try to convince Aunty on that point; she has taken a fancy to Pat and won't see any fault in her. She's a good enough child, but I can't get anything out of her; she is so odd and shy."

"I can! She's first rate and takes care of me better than anyone else," said Harry, the lame boy, with sudden warmth. Patty had quite won his selfish little heart by many services.

"She'll make Mother a nice helper as she grows up, and I consider it a good speculation. In four years, she'll be eighteen, and if she goes on doing so well, I won't begrudge her wages," added Mr. Murray, who sat nearby with a small son on each knee.

+ + + + + + + + + + + + ✳ + + + + + + + + + + + +

"She'd be quite pretty if she were straight and plump and jolly. But she is as sober as a deacon, and when her work is done, she sits in a corner watching us with big eyes as shy and mute as a mouse," said Ned, the big brother, lounging on the sofa.

"A dull, steady-going girl, suited for a servant and no more," concluded Mrs. Murray, setting down her cup as if the subject were closed.

"You are quite mistaken, and I'll prove it!" Aunt Jane announced, jumping up so energetically that the boys laughed and the elders looked annoyed. Pulling out a portfolio, Aunt Jane untied a little bundle of letters, saying impressively—

"Now listen, all of you, and see what has been going on with Patty this year."

Then Miss Jane read the little letters one by one, and it was curious to see how the faces of the listeners first grew attentive, then touched, then self-reproachful, and finally filled with interest and respect and something very like affection for little Patty.

+ + + + + + + + + + + + ✳ + + + + + + + + + + + +

These letters were pathetic, read as Aunty read them to listeners who could supply much that the writer generously left unsaid, and the involuntary comments of the hearers proved the truth of Patty's words.

"Does she envy me because I'm pretty and gay and have a good time? I never thought how hard it must be for her to see me have all the fun and she all the work. She's a girl like me and I might have done more for her than give her my old clothes and let her help me get dressed for parties," said Ella hastily as Aunt Jane laid aside one letter in which poor Patty told of many "good times and she not in 'em."

"Sakes alive! If I'd known the child wanted me to kiss her now and then as I do the rest, I'd have done it in a minute!" said Mrs. Murray, with sudden softness in her sharp eyes as Aunt Jane read this little bit—

"I am grateful, but, oh! I'm so lonely, and it's so hard not to have any mother like the other children. If Mrs. Murray would only kiss me goodnight sometimes, it would do me more good than pretty clothes or nice food."

"I've been thinking I'd let her go to school ever since I heard her showing Bob how to do his lessons. But Mother didn't think she could spare her," broke in Mr. Murray apologetically.

"If Ella would help a little, I guess I could allow it. Anyway, we might try for awhile, since she is so eager to learn," added his wife, anxious not to seem unjust in Jane's eyes.

"Well, Joe laughed at her as much as I did when the boys hunched up their shoulders the way she does," cried conscious-stricken Bob, who had just heard a sad little paragraph about her crooked figure and learned that it came from lugging heavy babies at the orphanage.

"I cuffed 'em both for it, and I have always liked Patty," said Harry, in a moral tone, which moved Ned to say—

"You'd be a selfish little rascal if you didn't, when she slaves so for you and gets no thanks for it. Now that I know how it tires her poor little back to carry wood and water, I shall do it myself, of course. If she'd only told me, I'd have done it all the time."

And so it went until the letters were done and they knew Patty as she was. Each felt sorry that he or she had not found her out before. Aunt Jane freed her mind on the subject, but the others continued to discuss it until quite an enthusiastic state of feeling set in and Patty was in danger of being killed with kindness.

It is astonishing how generous and clever people are when once awakened to duty, a charity, or a wrong. Now everyone was eager to repair past neglect, and if Aunt Jane had not wisely restrained them, the young folks would have done something absurd.

They laid many nice little plans to surprise Patty, and each privately resolved not only to give her a Christmas gift but also to do the better thing by turning over a new leaf for the new year.

+ + + + + + + + + + + + ＊ + + + + + + + + + + + +

The Family Comes Home

All the way home, they talked over their various projects and the boys kept bouncing into the seat with Aunt Jane to ask advice about their funny ideas.

"It must have been rather lonesome for the poor little soul all day. I declare, I wish we'd taken her along!" said Mrs. Murray, as they approached the house through the softly falling snow.

"She's got a jolly good fire all ready for us, and that's a mercy, for I'm half frozen," said Harry, hopping up the step.

"Don't you think if I touch up my blue merino, it would fit Patty and make a nice dress along with one of my white aprons?" whispered Ella, as she helped Aunt Jane out of the sleigh.

"I hope the child isn't sick or scared. It's two hours later than I expected to be home," added Mr. Murray, stepping up to peep in at the kitchen window for no one came to open the door and no light but the blaze of the fire shone out.

"Come softly and look in," he whispered, beckoning to the rest. "It's a pretty little sight even if it is in a kitchen."

Quietly creeping to the two low windows, they all looked in, and no one said a word, for the lonely little figure was both pretty and pathetic when they remembered the letters lately read. Patty lay flat on the old rug, fast asleep with one arm pillowed under her head. In the other arm lay Puss in a cozy bunch, as if she had crept there to be sociable since there was no one else to share Patty's long vigil. A row of slippers, large and small, stood warming on the hearth, two little nightgowns hung over

+ + + + + + + + + + + + + ✳ + + + + + + + + + + + + +

a chair, the teapot stood in a warm nook, and through the open door, they could see the lamp burning brightly in the sitting room, the table ready, and all things in order.

"Faithful little creature! She's thought of every blessed thing, and I'll go right in and wake her with a good kiss!" cried Mrs. Murray, darting for the door.

But Aunt Jane drew her back, begging her not to frighten the child by any sudden, unexpected demonstrations of affection. So they all went softly in—so softly that tired Patty did not wake, even though Puss pricked up her ears and opened her moony eyes with a lazy purr.

"Look here!" whispered Bob, pointing to the poor little gifts half tumbling out of Patty's apron. She had been pinning names on them when she fell asleep, and now her secret was known too soon.

No one laughed at the presents, and with a look of tender pity, Ella covered the few humble treasures in Patty's box. As she laid back, she remembered what she had once called "rubbish," how full her own boxes were with the pretty things girls love, and how easy it would have been to add to Patty's pitiful store.

No one exactly knew how to awaken the sleeper for she was something more than a servant in their eyes now. Aunt Jane settled the matter by stooping down and taking Patty in her arms. The big eyes opened at once and stared up at the face above. Then a smile so bright, so glad, shone all over the child's face as she clung to Aunt Jane, crying joyously—

"Is it really you? I was so afraid you wouldn't come that I cried myself to sleep."

Never before had any of them seen such love and happiness in Patty's face, heard such a glad, tender sound in her voice, or guessed what an ardent soul dwelt in her quiet body.

She was herself again in a minute, and jumping up, slipped away to see that everything was ready should anyone want supper after the cold drive.

Soon the family went off to bed and there was no time to let out the secret. Patty was surprised by the kind goodnights everyone sent her way, but she thought no more of it than to feel that Miss Jane brought a warmer atmosphere to the home.

A Place
for Patty

Patty's surprise began early the next day for the first thing she saw upon opening her eyes was a pair of new stockings crammed full of gifts hanging at the foot of her bed and several parcels lying on the table.

What a good time she had opening the delightful bundles. She laughed and cried at the droll things the boys gave and the comfortable and pretty things the elders sent. Such a happy child was she that when she tried to say her prayers, she couldn't find words beautiful enough to express her gratitude for so much kindness!

A new Patty went downstairs that morning—a bright-faced girl with smiles on the mouth that used to be so sad and silent, confidence in the timid eyes, and the magic of the heartiest goodwill to make her step light, her hand skillful, her labor a joy, and service no burden.

They do care for me, after all, and I never will complain again, she thought with a glad flutter at her heart and sudden color in her cheeks as everyone welcomed her with a friendly, "Merry Christmas, Patty!"

It was the merriest Christmas ever, and when the bountiful dinner was spread and Patty stood ready to wait, you can imagine her feelings as Mr. Murray pointed to a seat near Miss Jane and said in a fatherly tone that made his gruff voice sweet—

"Sit down and enjoy it with us, my girl; nobody has more right to it, and we are all one family today."

Patty could not eat much, her heart was so full, but it was a splendid feast to her, and when toasts were drunk she was overwhelmed by the honor Harry did her for he bounced up and exclaimed: "Now we must drink to 'Our Patty'—long life and good luck to her!"

That really was too much, and she fairly ran away to hide her blushes in the kitchen and work off her excitement washing dishes.

More surprises came that evening. When she went to put on her clean calico smock, she found the pretty blue dress and white apron laid ready on her bed along with a note that read, "With Ella's love."

"It's like a fairy story that keeps getting nicer and nicer since the godmother came," whispered Patty, as she glanced shyly at Aunt Jane.

"Christmas is the time for all sorts of pleasant miracles," answered Aunt Jane, smiling back at her little maiden, who looked so neat and blithe in her new dress and happy face.

Patty thought nothing further in the way of bliss could happen to her that night, but it did when Ned, anxious to atone for his past neglect, pranced up to her as a final dance was forming and said heartily—

+ + + + + + + + + + + + + * + + + + + + + + + + + +

"Come, Patty, everyone is to dance this one, even Harry and the cat!" And before she could collect her wits enough to say "No," she was leading off and flying down the middle with the young master, in great style.

That was the crowning honor, for she was a girl with all a girl's innocent hopes, fears, desires, and delights, and it had been rather hard to stand by while all the young neighbors were frolicking together.

Patty
Remembers

When everyone was gone, the tired children asleep, and the elders on their way up to bed, Mrs. Murray suddenly remembered she had not covered the kitchen fire. Aunt Jane said she would do it, and went down so softly that she did not disturb faithful Patty, who had also gone to see that all was safe.

Aunt Jane stopped to watch the little figure standing on the hearth alone, looking into the embers with thoughtful eyes. If Patty could have seen her future there, she would have found a long life spent in glad service to those she loved and who loved her. Not a splendid future, but a useful, happy one—

"only a servant" perhaps, yet a good and faithful woman, blessed with the confidence,
respect, and affection of those who knew her
genuine worth.

As a smile broke over Patty's face, Miss
Jane said with an arm round the little blue-
gowned figure—

"What are you dreaming and smiling about,
deary? The friends that are to come for you
someday, with a fine fortune in their pockets?"

"No ma'am, I feel as if I've found my folks.
I don't want any finer fortune than the love
they've given me today. I'm trying to think
how I can deserve it, and smiling because it's so
beautiful and I'm so happy," answered Patty,
looking up at her first friend with full eyes and
a glad glance that made her lovely.

THE END

***

Tilly's Christmas

C. M. DUDASH

Tilly's Christmas

"I'm so glad tomorrow is Christmas because I'm going to have lots of presents," said Kate, glowing with anticipation.

"I'm glad as well," Bessy chimed, "though I don't expect any presents but a pair of mittens."

It was Tilly's turn to speak, and she startled them with her words, "I'm very glad tomorrow is Christmas, even though I shan't have any presents at all."

These sentiments were spoken as the three little girls trudged home from school, and Tilly's words struck a cord of pity in the others. Kate and Bessy wondered how she could speak so cheerfully and be so happy when she was too poor to receive even the smallest of gifts on Christmas Day.

"Don't you wish you could find a purse full of money right here in the path?" asked Kate, the child who was going to have lots of presents.

"Oh, don't I! If I could keep it honestly, that is," said Tilly, her eyes glowing at the prospect.

"What would you buy?" asked Bessy, rubbing her cold hands and longing for her mittens.

"I've worked it all out in my mind," Tilly responded. "I'd buy a pair of large, warm blankets, a load of wood, a shawl for mother, and a pair of shoes for me. If there was enough left, I'd give Bessy a new hat so that she would not have to wear Ben's old felt one."

The girls giggled at that, but Bessy pulled the funny hat down over her ears and said she was much obliged but she would rather have candy.

"Let's look, and maybe we can find a purse.

People are always going about with money at Christmastime. How do we know someone has not lost it here on this path?" said Kate.

So the three little girls went along the snowy road, looking about them, half in earnest, half in fun. Suddenly, Tilly sprang forward, exclaiming loudly, "I see it! I've found a purse!"

Kate and Bessy followed quickly, but sputtered with disappointment as they realized that there was no purse lying in the snow but only a little bird. It lay upon the snow with its wings spread and feebly fluttered, too weak to fly. Its little feet were benumbed with cold and its once bright eyes were dull with pain. Instead of a chipper song, it could only utter a faint chirp now and then as if pleading for help.

"Nothing but a stupid old robin. How maddening!" cried Kate, sitting down to rest on a nearby tree stump.

"I shan't touch it. I found one once and

took care of it until it was well. The ungrateful thing flew away the minute it was able," said Bessy, creeping under Kate's shawl and pulling her hands up under her chin to warm them.

Tilly heard not a word. "Poor little birdie!" she crooned. "How pitiful you look and how glad you must be to see someone coming along to help you. I'll take you up gently, and carry you home to mother. Don't be frightened, dear. I am your friend." Tilly knelt down in the snow, stroking the bird with her hand and the tenderest pity in her face.

It was only then that she realized Kate and Bessy were laughing.

"Don't stop for that thing," they chided. "Now come along. Let's continue looking for a purse before it gets too cold and dark."

"You wouldn't leave it to die!" cried Tilly. "I'd rather have the bird than the money we might find in a purse. After all, the purse would not be mine and I would only be tempted to keep it, but this poor little creature will thank and love me for my trouble. Thank goodness I came in time."

Gently lifting the bird, Tilly felt its tiny cold claws cling to her hand and its dim eyes brighten as it nestled down with a grateful chirp.

"Now I've a Christmas present after all," she said smiling. "I've always wanted a bird, and this one will be such a pretty pet for me."

"He'll fly away the first chance he gets and die anyhow," said Bessy. "You'd be better off not to waste your time with him."

"He can't pay you for taking care of him, and my mother says it isn't worthwhile to help folks that can't help us," added Kate.

"My mother said, 'Do to others as you would to be done to by them,' and I'm sure I'd like someone to help me if I was dying of cold and hunger. I also remember the little saying, 'Love your neighbor as yourself.' This bird is my little neighbor, and I'll love him and care for him, just as I often wish our rich neighbor would love and care for us," answered Tilly. She leaned forward slightly, breathing her warm breath over the tiny bird, who looked up at her with confiding eyes, quick to feel and know a friend.

"What a funny girl you are," said Kate. "Caring for that silly bird, and talking about loving your neighbor in that serious way. Mr. King doesn't care a bit for you and he never will, though he knows how poor you are, so I don't think your plan amounts to much."

"I believe it, and I shall be happy to do my part," answered Tilly. "I must bid you goodnight now and I hope you'll have a merry Christmas and receive lots of lovely things."

As she left her friends and walked on alone toward the little old house where she lived, Tilly's spirits began to sink. Suddenly, she felt so poor. Her eyes were filled with tears as she thought of all the pretty things other children would be finding in their stockings on Christmas morning. It would have been so pleasant to think of finding something for herself and pleasanter still to have been able to give her mother something nice. So many comforts were lacking with no hope of getting them. The little family was pressed enough to simply find food and firewood.

"Never mind, birdie," whispered Tilly. "We'll make the best of what we have and be merry in spite of our lack. You shall have a happy Christmas, anyway, and I know God won't forget us, even if everyone else does."

Tilly stopped a moment to dry her eyes and lean her cheek against the bird's soft breast. The tiny creature afforded her much comfort, though it could only love her, not one thing more.

"See, Mother, what a nice present I've found," she cried, entering the house with a cheery face that was like sunshine in the dark room.

+ + + + + + + + + + + + + ✳ + + + + + + + + + + + + +

"I'm glad of that, Dearie, as I have not been able to get my little girl anything but a rosy apple. What a poor little bird it is. Here, quickly, give the poor thing some of your warm bread and milk."

"Why Mother, this bowl is so full. I'm afraid you gave me all the milk," said Tilly, smiling over the nice, steaming supper that stood ready for her.

"I've had plenty, dear. Sit down and warm your feet. You may put the bird in my basket on this cozy flannel."

After placing the bird tenderly into the basket, Tilly peeped into the closet and saw nothing there but dry bread.

"Oh dear," Tilly exclaimed to herself, "Mother's given me all the milk and is going without her tea because she knows I'm hungry. I'll surprise her by fixing her a good supper while she is outside splitting wood."

As soon as her mother left the room, Tilly

reached for the old teapot and carefully poured out a part of the milk. Then from her pocket, she drew a great, plump bun that one of the school children had given her. She had saved it for just this purpose. She toasted a slice of the bun and set a bit of butter on the plate for her to put on it. When her mother came in, she found the table drawn up in a warm place, a hot cup of tea ready, and Tilly and the birdie waiting patiently.

Such a poor little supper, and yet such a happy one, for love, charity, and contentment were welcome guests around the humble table. That Christmas eve was a sweeter one even than that at the great house, where light shone, fires blazed, a great tree glittered, music sounded, and children danced and played.

"We must go to bed early," said Tilly's mother as they sat by the fire. "We must save the wood, for there is only enough to last through tomorrow. The day after, I shall be paid for my work, and we can buy more."

"If only my bird were a fairy bird and would give us three wishes," Tilly said quietly. "How nice that would be! But, the poor dear can give me nothing, and it is of no matter." Tilly was looking at the robin, who lay in the basket with his head under his wing, nothing more than a feathery little ball.

"He can give you one thing, Tilly," her mother said. "He can give you the pleasure of doing good. That is one of the sweetest things in life, and it can be enjoyed by the poor as well as the rich." As Tilly's mother spoke, she softly stroked her daughter's hair with her tired hand.

Suddenly Tilly started with surprise and pointed toward the window. "I saw a face—a man's face," she confided in a frightened whisper. "He was looking in. He's gone now, but I truly saw him."

Tilly's mother stood up and went to the

door. "Some traveler attracted by the light perhaps," she said.

The wind blew cold, the stars shone bright, the snow lay white on the field and the wood, and the Christmas moon was glittering in the sky, but no human person was standing within sight.

"What sort of face was it?" asked Tilly's mother, quickly closing the door.

"A pleasant sort of face, I think, but I was so startled to see it there that I don't quite know what it was like. I wish we had a curtain there," said Tilly.

"I like to have our light shine out in the evening, for the road is dark and lonely just here and the twinkle of our lamp is pleasant to people as they pass by. We can do so little for our neighbors. I am glad we can at least cheer them on their way," said Tilly's mother. "Now put those poor old shoes to dry and go to bed, dearie. I'll be coming soon."

+ + + + + + + + + + + + + ✳ + + + + + + + + + + + + +

Tilly went, taking her birdie with her to sleep in his basket near her bed, lest he should be lonely in the night. Soon the little house was dark and still.

When Tilly came down and opened the front door that Christmas morning, she gave a loud cry, clapped her hands together, and then stood still, quite speechless with wonder and delight. There, near the stoop, lay a great pile of firewood all ready to be burned. There was also a large bundle and a basket with a lovely nosegay of winter roses, holly, and evergreen tied to the handle.

"Oh Mother! Who could have left it?" cried Tilly, pale with excitement and the surprise of it all. She stepped out to bring in the basket, and her mother, a few steps behind, stooped down to scoop up the bundle.

"The best and dearest of all Christmas angels is called 'Charity,'" Tilly's mother answered, her eyes welling with tears as she undid the bundle. "She walks abroad at Christmastime doing beautiful deeds like this, and never staying to be thanked."

It was all there—all that Tilly had imagined. There were warm, thick blankets, the comfortable shawl, a pair of new shoes, and best of all, a pretty winter hat for Bessy. The basket was full of good things to eat, and on the flowers lay a small note saying, "For the little girl who loves her neighbor as herself."

"Mother, I really do think my little bird is an angel in disguise and that all these splendid things came from him," said Tilly, laughing and crying with joy.

It really did seem so. As Tilly spoke, the robin flew to the table, hopped to the nosegay, and perching among the roses, began to chirp with all his little might. The sun streamed in on the flowers, the tiny bird, and the happy child with her mother. No one saw a shadow glide across the window or ever knew that Mr.

King had seen and heard the little girls the night before. No one ever dreamed that the rich neighbor had learned a priceless lesson from his poor little neighbor girl.

And Tilly's bird was a Christmas angel, for by the love and tenderness she gave to the helpless little creature, she brought good gifts to herself, happiness to an unknown benefactor, and the faithful friendship of a little friend who did not fly away, but stayed with her until the snow was gone, making summer for her in the wintertime.

THE END

✦ ✦

Rosa's Tale

Rosa's Tale

"Now, I believe everyone has had a Christmas present and a good time. Nobody has been forgotten, not even the cat," said Mrs. Ward to her daughter, as she looked at Pobbylinda, purring on the rug, with a new ribbon round her neck and the remains of a chicken bone between her paws.

It was very late, for the Christmas tree was decorated, the little folks in bed, the baskets and bundles left at poor neighbors' doors, and everything ready for the happy day which would begin as the clock struck twelve. They were resting after their mother's words reminded Belinda of one good friend who had received no gift that night.

"We've forgotten Rosa! Her mistress is away, but she shall have a present nevertheless. As late as it is, I know she would like some apples and cake and a Merry Christmas from the family."

Belinda jumped up as she spoke, and having collected such remnants of the feast as a horse would relish, she put on her hood, lighted a lantern, and trotted off to the barn to deliver her Christmas cheer.

As she opened the door of the loose box in which Rosa was kept, Belinda saw Rosa's eyes shining in the dark as she lifted her head with a startled air. Then, recognizing a friend, the horse rose and came rustling through the straw to greet her late visitor. She was evidently much pleased with the attention and gratefully rubbed her nose against Miss Belinda. At the same time, she poked her nose suspiciously into the contents of the basket.

Miss Belinda well knew that Rosa was an unusually social beast and would enjoy the little feast more if she had company, so she hung up the lantern, and sitting down on an inverted bucket, watched her as she munched contentedly.

"Now really," said Miss Belinda, when telling her story afterwards, "I am not sure whether I took a nap and dreamed what follows, or whether it actually happened, for strange things do occur at Christmastime, as everyone knows.

"As I sat there the town clock struck twelve, and the sound reminded me of the legend, which affirms that all dumb animals are endowed with speech for one hour after midnight on Christmas eve, in memory of the animals who lingered near the manger when the blessed Christ Child was born.

"I wish this pretty legend were true and our Rosa could speak, if only for an hour. I'm sure she has an interesting history, and I long to know all about it.

"I said this aloud, and to my utter amazement

the bay mare stopped eating, fixed her intelligent eyes upon my face, and answered in a language I understood perfectly well—'You shall indeed know my history, for whether the legend you mention is true or not, I do feel that I can confide in you and tell you all that I feel,' sweet Rosa told me.

"'I was lying awake listening to the fun in the house, thinking of my dear mistress so far away across the ocean and feeling very sad, for I heard you say that I was to be sold. That nearly broke my heart for no one has ever been so kind to me as Miss Merry, and nowhere shall I be taken care of, nursed, and loved as I have been since she bought me. I know I'm getting old and stiff in the knees. My forefoot is lame, and sometimes I'm cross when my shoulder aches; but I do try to be a patient, grateful beast. I've gotten fat with good living, my work is not hard, and I dearly love to carry those who have done so much for me; I'll carry them about until I die in the harness if they will only keep me.'

"I was so astonished by Rosa's speech that I tumbled off the pail on which I was sitting and landed in the straw staring up at Rosa, as dumb as if I had lost the power she had gained. She seemed to enjoy my surprise, and added to it by letting me hear a genuine horse laugh, hearty, shrill, and clear, as she shook her pretty head and went on talking rapidly in the language which I now perceived to be a mixture of English and the peculiar dialect of the horse country.

*

83

*

"'Thank you for remembering me tonight, and in return for the goodies you bring I'll tell my story as quickly as I can, for I have often longed to recount the trials and triumphs of my life. Miss Merry came last Christmas eve to bring me sugar, and I wanted to speak, but it was too early and I could not say a word, though my heart was full.'

"Rosa paused an instant, and her fine eyes dimmed as if with tender tears at the recollection of the happy year, which followed the day she was bought from the drudgery of a livery stable to be a lady's special pet. I stroked her neck as she stooped to sniff affectionately at my hood, and eagerly said—

"'Tell away, dear, I'm full of interest, and understand every word you say.'

"Thus encouraged, Rosa threw up her head, and began once again to speak with an air of pride, which plainly proved what we had always suspected, that she belonged to a good family.

"'My father was a famous racer, and I am very like him; the same color, spirit, and grace, and but for the cruelty of man, I might have been as renowned as he. I was a happy colt, petted by my master, tamed by love, and never struck a blow while he lived. I won one race for him, and my future seemed so promising that when he died, I brought a great price.

"'I mourned the death of my master, but I was glad to be sent to my new owner's racing stable, where I was made over by everyone. I heard many predictions that I would be another Goldsmith Maid or Flora Temple. Ah, how ambitious and proud I was in those days! I was truly vain in regard to my good blood, my speed, and my beauty; for indeed, I was handsome then, though you may find it difficult to believe now.' Rosa sighed regretfully as she stole a look at me, and turned her head in a way that accentuated the fine lines about her head and neck.

"'I do not find it hard to believe at all,' I answered. 'Miss Merry saw them, though you seemed to be nothing more than a skeleton when she bought you. The Cornish blacksmith who shod you noted the same. It is easy to see that you belong to a good family by the way you hold your head without a check-rein and carry your tail like a plume,' I said, with a look of admiration.

"'I must hurry over this part of my story because, though brilliant, it was very brief, and ended in a way that made it the bitterest portion of my life,' continued Rosa. 'I won several races and everyone predicted that I would earn great fame. You may guess how high my reputation was when I tell you that before my last fatal trial thousands were bet on me, and my rival trembled at the thought of racing against me.

"'I was full of spirit, eager to show my speed and sure of success. Alas, how little I knew of the wickedness of human nature then, how dearly I bought the knowledge, and how completely it has changed my whole life! You do not know much about such matters, of course, and I won't digress to tell you all the tricks of the trade; only beware of jockeys and never bet.

"'I was kept carefully out of everyone's way for weeks and only taken out for exercise by my trainer. Poor Bill! I was fond of him, and he was so good to me that I never have forgotten him, though he broke his neck years ago. A few nights before the great race, as I was enjoying a good sleep carefully tucked away in my stall, someone stole in and gave me a dish of warm mash. It was dark, and I was but half awake. I ate it like a fool, even though I knew by instinct that it was not Bill who left it for me.

"'I was a trusting creature then, and used to all sorts of strange things being done to prepare me to race. For that reason, I never suspected that something could be wrong. Something was very wrong, however, and the deceit of it has caused me to be suspicious of any food ever since. You see, the mash was dosed in some way; it made me very ill and nearly allowed my enemies to triumph. What a shameful, cowardly trick.

"'Bill worked with me day and night, trying desperately to prepare me to run. I did my best to seem well, but there was not time for me to regain my lost strength and spirit. My pride was the only thing that kept me going. "I'll win for my master even if I die in doing it," I said to myself. When the hour came, I pranced to my place trying to look as well as ever, though my heart was heavy and I trembled with excitement. "Courage, my lass, and we'll beat them in spite of their dark tricks," Bill whispered, as he sprang into place.

"'I lost the first heat, but won the second, and the sound of the cheering gave me strength to walk away without staggering, though my legs shook under me. What a splendid minute that was when, encouraged and refreshed by my faithful Bill, I came on the track again! I knew my enemies began to fear. I carried myself so bravely that they fancied I was quite well, and now, excited by that first success, I was mad with impatience to be off and cover myself with glory.'

"'Rosa looked as if her 'splendid moment' had come again, for she arched her neck, opened wide her red nostrils, and pawed the straw with one little foot. At the same time, her eyes shone with sudden fire, and her ears were pricked up as if to catch again the shouts of the spectators on that long ago day.

"'I wish I had been there to see you!' I exclaimed, quite carried away by her ardor.

"'I wish you had indeed,' she answered, 'for I won. I won! The big black horse did his best, but I had vowed to win or die, and I kept my word. For I beat him by a head, and as quickly as I had done so, I fell to the ground as if dead. I might as well have died then and there. I heard those around me whispering that the poison, the exercise, and the fall had ruined me as a racer.

"'My master no longer cared for me and would have had me shot if kind Bill had not saved my life. I was pronounced good for nothing and Bill was able to buy me cheaply. For quite a long time, I was lame and useless, but his patient care did wonders, and just as I was able to be of use to him, he was killed.

"'A gentleman in search of a saddle horse purchased me because my easy gait and quiet temper suited him; for I was meek enough now, and my size allowed me to carry his delicate daughter.

+ + + + + + + + + + + + + ✳ + + + + + + + + + + + + +

"'For more than a year, I served little Miss Alice, rejoicing to see how rosy her pale cheeks became, how upright her feeble figure grew, thanks to the hours she spent with me. My canter rocked her as gently as if she were in a cradle and fresh air was the medicine she needed. She often said she owed her life to me, and I liked to think so, for she made my life a very easy one.

"'But somehow my good times never lasted long, and when Miss Alice went west, I was sold. I had been so well treated that I looked as handsome and happy as ever. To be honest though, my shoulder never was strong again, and I often had despondent moods, longing for the excitement of the race track with the instinct of my kind; so I was glad when, attracted by my spirit and beauty, a young army officer bought me and I went to the war.

"'Ah! You never guessed that, did you? Yes, I did my part gallantly and saved my master's life more than once. You have observed how martial music delights me, but you don't know that it is because it reminds me of the proudest hour of my life. I've told you about the saddest—now listen as I tell you about the bravest and give me a pat for the courageous act that won my master his promotion though I got no praise for my part of the achievement.

"'In one of the hottest battles, my captain was ordered to lead his men on a most perilous mission. They hesitated, so did he, for it was certain to cost many lives, and, brave as they were, they paused an instant. But, I settled the point. Wild with the sound of drums, the smell of powder, and the excitement of the hour, I rebelled. Though I was sharply reined in, I took the bit between my teeth, and dashed straight ahead into the midst of the fight. Though he tried, my rider could do nothing to stop me. The men, thinking their captain was leading them on, followed cheering loudly and carrying all that was before them.

+ + + + + + + + + + + + + ✳ + + + + + + + + + + + + +

"'What happened just after that I never could remember, except that I got a wound here in my neck and a cut on my flank. The scar is there still, and I'm proud of it, though buyers always consider it a blemish. When the battle was won my master was promoted on the field, and I carried him up to the general as he sat among his officers under the torn flags.

"'Both of us were weary and wounded, both of us were full of pride at what we had done; but he received all the praise and honor. I received only a careless word and a better supper than usual.

"'It seemed so wrong that no one knew or appreciated my courageous action. Not a one seemed to care that it was the horse, not the man, who led that fearless charge. I did think I deserved at least a rosette—others received much more for far less dangerous deeds. My master alone knew the truth of the matter. He thanked me for my help by keeping me always with him until the sad day when he was killed in a skirmish and lay for hours with no one to watch and mourn over him but his faithful horse.

"'Then I knew how much he loved and thanked me. His hand stroked me while it had the strength, his eye turned to me until it grew too dim to see, and when help came at last, I heard him whisper to a comrade, "Be kind to Rosa and send her safely home. She has earned her rest."

"'I had earned it, but I did not get it. When I arrived home, I was received by a mother whose heart was broken by the loss of her son. She did not live long to cherish me. The worst of my bad times were only beginning.

"'My next owner was a fast young man who treated me badly in many ways. At last the spirit of my father rose within me and I ran away with my master and caused him to take a brutal fall.

"'To tame me down, I was sold as a carriage horse. That almost killed me, for it was dreadful drudgery. Day after day, I pulled heavy loads behind me over the hard pavement. The horses that pulled alongside me were far from friendly and there was no affection to cheer my life.

"'I have often longed to ask why Mr. Bergh does not try to prevent such crowds from piling into those carriages. Now I beg you to do what you can to stop such an unmerciful abuse.

"'In snowstorms it was awful, and more than one of my mates dropped dead with overwork and discouragement. I used to wish I could do the same, for my poor feet, badly shod, became so lame I could hardly walk at times, and the constant strain on the up-grades brought back the old trouble in my shoulder worse than ever.

"'Why they did not kill me, I don't know. I was a miserable creature then, but there must be something attractive that lingers about me for people always seem to think I am worth saving. Whatever can it be, ma'am?'

"'Now, Rosa, don't talk so. You know you

are an engaging little animal, and if you live to be forty, I'm sure you will still have certain pretty ways about you—ways that win the hearts of women, if not of men. Women sympathize with your afflictions, find themselves amused with your coquettish airs, and like your affectionate nature. Men, unfortunately, see your weak points and take a money view of the case. Now hurry up and finish. It's getting a bit cold out here.'

"I laughed as I spoke and Rosa eyed me with a sidelong glance and gently waved her docked tail, which was her delight. The sly thing liked to be flattered and was as fond of compliments as a girl.

"'Many thanks. I will come now to the most interesting portion of my narrative. As I was saying, instead of knocking me on the head, I was packed off to New Hampshire and had a fine rest among the green hills, with a dozen or so weary friends. It was during this holiday that I acquired the love of nature Miss Merry detected and liked in me when she found me ready to study sunsets with her, to admire new landscapes, and enjoy bright summer weather.

"'In the autumn, a livery stable keeper bought me, and through the winter, he fed me well. By spring, I was quite presentable. It was a small town, but a popular place to visit in the summertime. I was kept on the trot while the season lasted, mostly because ladies found me easy to drive. You, Miss Belinda, were one of the ladies, and I never shall forget, though I have long ago forgiven it, how you laughed at my odd gait the day you hired me.

"'My tender feet and stiff knees made me tread very gingerly and amble along with short mincing steps, which contrasted rather strangely with my proudly waving tail and high carried head. You liked me nevertheless because I didn't rattle you senseless as we traveled down the steep hills. You also seemed pleased that I didn't startle at the sight of locomotives and stood patiently while you gathered flowers and enjoyed the sights and sounds.

"'I have always felt a regard for you because you did not whip me and admired my eyes, which, I may say without vanity, have always been considered unusually fine. But no one ever won my whole heart like Miss Merry, and I never shall forget the happy day when she came to the stable to order a saddle horse. Her cheery voice caught my attention and when she said after looking at several showy beasts, "No, they don't suit me. This little one here has the right air," my heart danced within me and I looked 'round with a whinny of delight. "Can I ride her?" she asked, understanding my welcome. She came right up to me, patted me, peered into my face, rubbed my nose, and looked at my feet with an air of interest and sympathy that made me feel as if I'd like to carry her clear around the world.

"'Ah, what rides we had after that! What happy hours trotting merrily through the green woods, galloping over the breezy hills, and pacing slowly along quiet lanes, where I often lunched luxuriously on clover tops while Miss Merry took a sketch of some picturesque scene with me in the foreground.

"'I liked that very much. We had long chats at such times, and I was convinced that she understood me perfectly. She was never frightened when I danced for pleasure on the soft turf. She never chided me when I snatched a bite from the young trees as we passed through sylvan ways, never thought it any trouble to let me wet my tired feet in babbling brooks, and always kindly dismounted long enough to remove the stones that plagued me.

"'Then how well she rode! So firm yet light in the seat, so steady a hand on the reins, so agile a foot to spring on and off, and such infectious spirits. No matter how despondent or cross I might be, I felt happy and young again whenever dear Miss Merry was on my back.'

"Here Rosa gave a frisk that sent the straw

flying and made me shrink into a corner. She pranced about the box, neighing so loudly that she woke the big brown colt in the next stall and set poor Buttercup to lowing for her lost calf, which she had managed to forget about for a few moments in sleep.

"'Ah, Miss Merry never ran away from me! She knew my heels were to be trusted, and she let me play as I would, glad to see me lively. Never mind, Miss Belinda, come out and I'll behave as befits my years,' laughed Rosa, composing herself, and adding in a way so like a woman that I could not help smiling in the dark—

"'When I say "years," I beg you to understand that I am not as old as that base man declared, but just in the prime of life for a horse. Hard usage has made me seem old before my time, but I am good for years of service yet.'

"'Few people have been through as much as you have, Rosa, and you certainly have

earned the right to rest.' I said consolingly, for her little whims and vanities amused me.

"'You know what happened next,' she continued, 'but I must seize this opportunity to express my thanks for all the kindness I've received since Miss Merry bought me, in spite of the ridicule and dissuasion of all her friends.

"'I know I didn't look a good bargain. I was very thin and lame and shabby, but she saw and loved the willing spirit in me. She pitied my hard lot and felt that it would be a good deed to buy me even if she never got much work out of me.

"'I shall always remember that, and whatever happens to me hereafter, I never shall be as proud again as I was the day she put my new saddle and bridle on me. I was led out, sleek, plump, and handsome with blue rosettes at my ears, my tail cut in the English style, and on my back, Miss Merry sat in her London hat and habit, all ready to head a cavalcade of eighteen horsemen and horsewomen.

"'We were the most perfect pair of all, and when the troop pranced down the street six abreast, my head was the highest, my rider the straightest, and our two hearts the friendliest in all the goodly company.

"'Nor is it pride and love alone that bind me to her. It is gratitude as well. She often bathed my feet herself, rubbed me down, watered me, blanketed me, and came daily to see me when I was here alone for weeks in the winter. Didn't she write to the famous friend of my race for advice, and drive me seven miles to get a good smith to shoe me well? Didn't she give me weeks of rest without shoes in order to save my poor contracted feet? And am I not now fat and handsome, and barring the stiff knees, a very presentable horse? If I am, it is all owing to Miss Merry, and for that reason, I want to live and die in her service.

"'She doesn't want to sell me and only told you to do so because you didn't want to care for me while she is gone. Dear Miss Belinda, please keep me! I'll eat as little as I can. I won't ask for a new blanket, though this old army one is thin and shabby. I'll trot for you all winter and try not to show it if I am lame. I'll do anything a horse can, no matter how humble, in order to earn my living. Don't, I beg you, send me away among strangers who have neither interest nor pity for me!'

"Rosa had spoken rapidly, feeling that her plea must be made now or never. Before another Christmas, she might be far away and speech of no use to win her wish. I was greatly touched, even though she was only a horse. She was looking earnestly at me as she spoke and made the last words very eloquent by preparing to bend her stiff knees and lie down at my feet. I stopped her and answered with an arm about her neck and her soft nose in my hand—

"'You shall not be sold, Rosa! You shall go and board at Mr. Town's great stable, where you will have pleasant society among the eighty horses who usually pass the winter there. Your shoes shall be taken off so that you might rest until March at least. Your care will be only the best, my dear, and I will come and see you. In the spring, you shall return to us, even if Miss Merry is not here to welcome you.'

"'Thanks, many, many thanks! But I wish I could do something to earn my board. I hate to be idle, though rest is delicious. Is there nothing I can do to repay you, Miss Belinda? Please answer quickly. I know the hour is almost over,' cried Rosa, stamping with anxiety. Like all horses, she wanted the last word.

"'Yes, you can,' I cried, as a sudden idea popped into my head. 'I'll write down what you have told me and send the little story to a certain paper I know of. The money I get for it will pay your board. So rest in peace, my dear. You will have earned your living after all and you may rest knowing that your debt is paid.'

"Before she could reply, the clock struck one. A long sigh of satisfaction was all the response in her power. But, we understood each other now, and cutting a lock from her hair for Miss Merry, I gave Rosa a farewell caress and went on my way. I couldn't help wondering if I had made it all up or the charming beast had really broken a year's silence and freed her mind.

"However that may be, here is the tale. The sequel to it is that the bay mare has really gone to board at a first-class stable," concluded Miss Belinda. "I call occasionally and leave my card in the shape of an apple, finding Madam Rosa living like an independent lady, her large box and private yard on the sunny side of the barn, a kind ostler to wait upon her, and much genteel society from the city when she is inclined for company.

"What more could any reasonable horse desire?"

THE END

+ + + + + + + + + + + + + + + + * + + + + + + + + + + + + + +

The Editor's Notes

The Quiet Little Woman—

The world of Patty, the orphan girl, was one with which Louisa May Alcott was quite familiar. Louisa's mother had been one of the first paid social workers in the United States, and all of the Alcott family had a strong sense of social obligation. By the standards of their day, they would have been regarded as quite progressive in their views, and many times they showed themselves ready to help those in need even as they had been helped in their impecunious days.

Nevertheless, Louisa May Alcott would have found it strange indeed if anyone had suggested to her that there could be a general scheme for helping all in need regardless of an individual's efforts and personal morality. She herself had put forth Herculean efforts to write enough stories, including some rather gaudy thrillers, to pull the Alcott family out of debt. Naturally, she came to believe that individual effort made a difference.

In all her writing, Louisa's characters exhibit virtue and vice within a context of personal responsibility. Characters like poor Patty may indeed need a helping hand from someone like Aunt Jane—especially at Christmastime—but Patty must help too. She has powers of her own and a will of her own that she must draw on to accept her lot and find happiness where she can.

No one could tell Miss Alcott about the nature of poverty and privation because she knew of it firsthand, and she also knew that there really were people in the world who had earned, or were worthy of, a second chance, while there were others, like the bad maid Lizzie Brown, who "deserved nothing" and squandered her chance at a good life.

Perhaps we today need to learn a lesson from Miss Alcott and from Patty. All too often we are told there is no limit to what we can do and what personal peace, comfort, and satisfaction we may achieve—if only hindrances to opportunity could be swept from our path, perhaps by the church, perhaps by a social organization, perhaps by the mercy of the government itself, regardless of whether we are worthy of the opportunity or not.

But for Patty and Louisa May, moral character cannot be excluded as a factor in our own well-being and in what we make of ourselves and of our opportunities. As we awaken morally to what is charitable, truthful, and good, we awaken our own souls to moral transformation. If we have been dealt a bad hand by life, the virtue of accepting what has been dealt to us strengthens us to our challenge. Others have overcome through worthy endeavors; so can we.

Christmas is a good time to ponder these truths. Charity is a theme of the season, yet how charity is received is important, too.

As Louisa May Alcott knew from her own observations, moral good is rewarded, often in this life, and surely in the world to come. Vice, on the other hand, gives us no aid in battling against the odds of going upstream. Most success and even peace is achieved by overcoming, and goodness helps us rise to our occasion and opportunity, no matter how rarely they might come.

True, it has been observed that sometimes the unworthy do prosper, but even that cannot take away from the satisfaction of virtue. For virtue itself is a reward, a prosperity to the soul, to be enjoyed equally by both the humble and the great.

Tilly's Christmas—

Louisa May Alcott's great gift as a writer revealed itself in her deft characterizations of her heroes and heroines. Sometimes using but a few words of dialogue, she could lay out the essential nature of a boy or a girl whose special thoughtfulness marked them out for praise and reward.

While Miss Alcott was not the only writer for children who believed that the kindly child would ultimately find kindness, and that generous children would surely find generosity returned, she may have been one of that philosophy's most convincing proponents.

Miss Alcott's own fairy tale life was characterized by early poverty and desperate illness, followed by unparalleled success as a writer. By the tender age of thirty-six, she had delivered her father, her mother, and her sisters from the utter penury of their early existence.

At the close of *Tilly's Christmas*, it is said of the main character "for by the love and tenderness she gave to the helpless . . . she brought good gifts to herself." Such was true of the amazing Louisa May Alcott. And such is true of her kind heroine.

Rosa's Tale—

Aesop may have originated the talking animal story, but he was by no means its last practitioner. Fables and moral tales featuring animals were popular throughout the Middle Ages, and even the famous English poet Geoffrey Chaucer had a thing or two to say about a rooster in Canterbury.

No one knows the origin of the story of animals being endowed with speech on Christmas Eve as a reward for their silence while the baby Jesus slept in a manger, but "Rosa's Tale" shows the true mettle of a horse who is given one great opportunity to speak for herself about the mistreatment she has suffered at human hands.

Christmas is the season of thoughtfulness; Belinda's response to Rosa's story is surely appropriate to the season. "Rosa's Tale" is worthy of even the great Chaucer's ingenuity as a moral tale.

ABOUT THE AUTHOR

Louisa May Alcott is the beloved author of one of the world's great classics of literature, *Little Women*. First published in 1868, *Little Women* has captured the imaginations of countless generations of young adults who thrill to read the seemingly real-life adventures of Meg, Jo, Beth, and Amy of the impoverished March family.

A groundbreaking work at the time, Miss Alcott's story is one of the first books to treat children as real people, with real feelings and varied motives, in a realistic setting. Miss Alcott's characters hope, sorrow, and strive in a way that makes readers care for and believe in them.

With the success of *Little Women*, Louisa May Alcott became established as one of the leading lights of American literature and one of the most successful authors of her time.

Although her fame was sudden, it did not come easily.

Born in 1832, Louisa May Alcott's fairy tale life did not have a fairy tale beginning. Her father, Bronson Alcott, was an earnest, impractical man who, without much formal education decided to become a schoolteacher and educational reformer. He failed in the educational profession several times, and with each failure came further poverty for his family. It was left to Louisa's mother, Abba Alcott, to give the family some semblance of emotional and financial stability.

Abba Alcott had to demonstrate a practicality that did not seem to dwell in the deep philosophical and educational recesses of Bronson Alcott's mind. Most assuredly the model for the character Marmee in *Little Women*, Abba became one of Boston's first social workers, and with her meager income, kept the family supplied as best she could with material necessities.

Abba's example of self-sacrifice greatly

affected her daughter. From a very early age, Louisa May began to act the role of an adult and took it upon herself to do what she could to pull her family out of genteel, and sometimes not so genteel, poverty. She took any menial job to help out and was very aware of the fact that friend and neighbor Ralph Waldo Emerson had made them gifts of money over the years.

From very early on, Louisa Alcott was able to help the family by publishing short articles, poems, and stories in the various magazines that fed the voracious reading appetite of the Boston public. While these efforts never paid great sums of money, they did provide a little relief for the family and a lot of experience for Louisa.

Ironically enough, it was the Civil War that gave Miss Alcott her freedom to step out of the family shadows and into her own limelight.

In 1862, Louisa May Alcott volunteered to become a nurse in a Union hospital. The experience, though short, changed her life. After the briefest of training, she found herself caring for desperately ill and dying men. She discovered new strength in herself as she fed her charges, helped alleviate their sufferings, and ministered words of comfort to those who would not see home nor sweetheart again.

The work was exhausting, the conditions for the nurses themselves appalling, and Louisa nearly died. Bronson Alcott himself had to come to Washington, D. C., to rescue her, and although she recovered rapidly, her health was never quite the same.

Out of this tragic experience came her war book, *Hospital Sketches*. In itself not a great success, the book did give evidence of a new maturity in Louisa's writing. This maturity was appreciated by her Boston publishers who became increasingly supportive of her work. Writing as much as thirty pages of copy a day, from this time forward, Miss Alcott never lacked an outlet for her writing.

Then, in 1868 came *Little Women*, instant

fame, and the enormous sum of $8,000 in roy-
alties. The family's financial worries were at an
end. The very happy conclusion of *Little Women*
really did mirror that of her own dear family
except for one thing: Louisa May Alcott never
married as Jo March did. That was a dream
that was never to be.

Instead, Louisa May remained faithful to
her family, nursing her mother through her last
illness, and finally passing away herself in the
same year her father died. From 1832 to 1888,
it had been a short but eventful life.

ABOUT THE PRESENTER

Stephen W. Hines is a writer, researcher, and editor who has worked with words on a professional basis for twenty years. His book, *Little House in the Ozarks: the Rediscovered Writings* (of Laura Ingalls Wilder), rose to the *Publishers Weekly* bestseller list in 1991. Since that time, he has devoted himself to the rediscovery of other worthy but overlooked efforts by famous authors.

Following several successful books on Laura Ingalls Wilder, Hines discovered *The Quiet Little Woman: A Christmas Story* by Louisa May Alcott in a long-forgotten children's magazine. It had lain unnoticed for more than seventy years. He hopes many new fans will be won to Louisa May Alcott through this charming tale.

Hines lives with his wife and daughters near Nashville, Tennessee, where he continues his research and writes a column for a local paper. His books have sold more than 350,000 copies.

If you have enjoyed this book,
or if it has impacted your life,
we would like to hear from you.
Please contact us at:

Honor Books
Department E
P.O. Box 55388
Tulsa, Oklahoma 74137
Or by e-mail at info@honorbooks.com

Additional copies of this book and other
titles by Honor Books are available
from your local bookstore.

Honor Books
Tulsa, Oklahoma